The GEORGE WASHINGTON
You Never Knew

BY JAMES LINCOLN COLLIER

Children's Press®
A Division of Scholastic Inc.
New York Toronto London Auckland Sydney
Mexico City New Delhi Hong Kong
Danbury, Connecticut

Library of Congress Cataloging-in-Publication Data

Collier, James Lincoln, 1928-
  The George Washington you never knew / by James Lincoln Collier;
illustrations by Greg Copeland.—1st American ed.
      p. cm.
Includes bibliographical references and index.
Summary: Explores the childhood, character, and influential events that
helped shape the life of the first president.
  ISBN 0-516-24343-8 (lib. bdg.)   0-516-25833-8 (pbk.)
  1. Washington, George, 1732-1799—Juvenile literature. 2. Presidents—
United States—Biography—Juvenile literature. [1.Washington, George,
1732-1799. 2. Presidents.] I. Copeland, Greg, ill.
II. Title.
  E312.66.C65 2003
  973.4'1'092—dc21

                              2003005248

Illustrations by Greg Copeland

Book design by A. Natacha Pimentel C.

Photographs © 2003: Art Resource, NY: 45 (National Portrait Gallery,
Wahington D.C.), 46 (Private Collection), 50 (Reunion des Musees
Nationaux), 56 (Reunion des Musees Nationaux /D. Arnaudet/G. Blot), 57
(Reunion des Musees Nationaux /RMN/P. Bernard), 33 (Reunion des Musees
Nationaux/El Meliani), 38 (Smithsonian American Art Museum, Washington
DC), 12 (The Pierpont Morgan Library/Joseph Zehavi), 65; Bridgeman Art
Library International Ltd., London/New York: 70 (Bristol City Museum and
Art Gallery, UK), 51 (Chateau Blerancourt, Picardy, France), 35 (Private
Collection); Corbis Images/The Corcoran Gallery of Art: cover, 1, 4; Courtesy
of the Mount Vernon Ladies Association: 31 bottom, 71, 73; North Wind
Picture Archives: 6, 7 , 10, 14, 19, 22, 23, 25, 29, 37, 41, 42, 48, 53, 58, 62,
66; The Art Archive/Picture Desk: 26 (General Wolfe Museum Quebec
House/Eileen Tweedy), 68 left, 68 right (National Gallery of Art
Washington/Album/Joseph Martin).

CONTENTS

Chapter 1

THE AMBITIOUS YOUNG MAN

THE GEORGE WASHINGTON WE KNOW—or think we know—is the man in a famous portrait with a solemn face. He is the stern-faced man in another famous painting, standing in the bow of the boat carrying him across the Delaware River, as if he were king. He is the Father of Our Country, not really a human being, but a godlike figure.

The real George Washington was an entirely different person. Warmhearted and generous, he would much rather be with people than study books.

This portrait of George Washington by Gilbert Stuart is one of the most famous of all American portraits. Copies have hung in thousands of classrooms, libraries, and offices.

When hard decisions had to be made, he would not go to the library but would gather people around him for lunch, dinner, or tea and ask for their opinions. He was basically religious, but he spent many more Sundays hunting foxes on horseback than he did in church. He had a weakness for fine clothes, handsome furniture, and good food and was always sending to London for a fashionable suit, a marble-topped table, or a gold-framed mirror. He liked to spend his evenings dancing, even gambling in card games.

He always found time to help out a friend or neighbor, giving them advice, lending them money, managing their estates after they died—to the point where he once said that he hardly had any time left for ordinary pleasures. Visitors streamed to his home at Mount Vernon, where they were warmly welcomed: he reported to a friend that he and his wife had not eaten dinner alone together for twenty years.

We can see from this why George Washington might be admired, even revered. We have trouble understanding that he might be loved. And yet he was. In 1783, when the American Revolution was winding down, a great many soldiers had gone unpaid. A group of army officers decided that they ought to march on the government, which was then in Philadelphia, and force it to give them their back pay.

George Washington liked having people around and was rarely without visitors to his famous home, Mount Vernon. Here, he and Martha say good-bye to a departing guest, who waves from the carriage window.

Washington was very disturbed. If the army decided to push the elected government around, it would be the end of democracy. Everything Americans had fought for would be lost.

Washington learned that a mass meeting of the officers had been called to make plans, so he called a meeting of his own. He spoke of how much he loved the soldiers he had fought with for so many years. But, he said, an attack on the government would mean an end to freedom, not only for them, but for their children and grandchildren. The officers would not back off.

Now Washington pulled out a letter he had received from a government official, saying that the government was trying to pay the money owed to the officers. He started to read it, but could not. Slowly he took out a pair of eyeglasses, which few of them had ever seen him wear.

"Gentlemen," he said, "You will permit me to put on my spectacles, for I have not only grown gray, but almost blind in the service of my country." The officers were so moved that some of them began to cry, so great was their love for their general. In that moment the rebellion was over: none of these tough warriors had the heart to go against Washington's wishes.

How, then, have we come to see Washington as a man of marble?

George Washington was born in Virginia, the oldest and the wealthiest of the English colonies in North America. His father was fairly well off, but was not one of the rich gentlemen who ran the colony of Virginia.

George's father had had two sons by a first marriage, and when his first wife died he married Mary Ball, who bore him several children. George was the eldest of this second batch of children. When he was eleven his father died. His mother,

Washington's mother, Mary Ball, was a very demanding woman who often wanted her son to pay attention to her when he was busy fighting the Revolution or running the government. But she gave him a sense of his own worth.

who doted on George, made him a sort of "captain" of his younger brothers and sister. He thus got a taste for command early in life.

With the death of George's father, the family finances went downhill. The Washingtons were by no means poor—they owned a lot of land and many slaves. But they could not keep up with many of the wealthy gentlemen and ladies they liked to mingle with. George was not able to go to school in England as his older half brothers had done. He thus started life feeling that he was behind in the race. He was determined he would not be behind for long.

He grew up to be very tall for that day, over six feet. He had reddish hair, great strength, and endurance. He was able to ride hour after hour around the Virginia countryside and into the wilderness filled with Indians in the western part of the state. He became an excellent horseman.

To make his way in the world he had to find a profession. At sixteen he settled on surveying. One of the main jobs of a surveyor was to measure and mark off land. So, surveyors usually got to know where the good pieces of land were, how much they were worth, and who owned them. Washington went into surveying with the idea of making money from buying and selling land.

This map shows Washington's path from Virginia into the Ohio Territory and up to Lake Erie, where he met with Indians and French army officers. It is based on Washington's own drawing of his route.

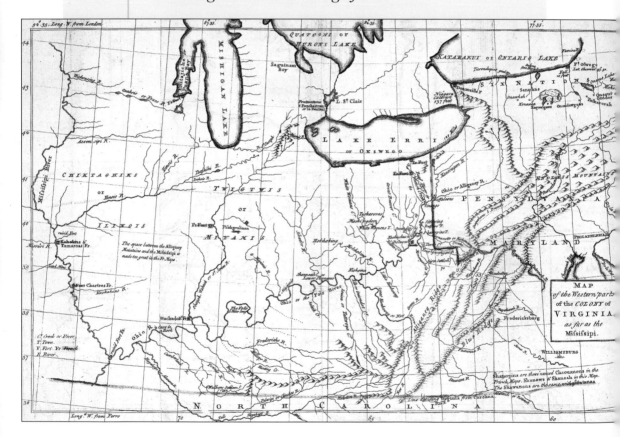

But the job led him down quite a different path. The so-called Ohio Territory, across the Allegheny Mountains, was worth a lot. This land was mostly covered with forest and filled with Indians. But it was very fertile and laced with rivers that eventually ran into the Mississippi and then out into the Gulf of Mexico. These rivers made a great natural transportation system by which goods from the area could be shipped out to the rest of America and Europe.

The French had been doing a very good business in furs, timber, and other products in Canada, often trading with the Indians for what they wanted. They hoped to expand into the Ohio Territory. The English, too, wanted to exploit the area. And the Americans in the thirteen colonies were eager to push over the mountains and carve out farms in this very fertile land. The soil in many parts of the original colonies was, after more than a century, growing thin.

The French held the little city of New Orleans at the mouth of the Mississippi River. If they could set up some forts along rivers in the Ohio Territory they could control much of the trade coming out of a huge section of North America. They were determined to do so. The stage was set for a showdown, which would thrust this obscure son of a quite unimportant Virginia family into the spotlight.

Chapter 2

HEADSTRONG IN THE WILDERNESS

GEORGE WASHINGTON'S JOB AS A surveyor took him into the wilderness at the western end of Virginia, a lot of which was still unsettled. He quickly discovered that he liked the rough life on the frontier, riding through hundreds of miles of forests, sleeping on the ground, eating whatever scraps of biscuit and dried meat he could carry in his pouches. He met Indians, watched them dance, learned their ways. He was still very young and inexperienced. But by the time he was twenty he had spent far more time in the wilderness than most colonists had.

An artist's idea of sixteen-year-old Washington surveying in the wilderness

In 1753 the British governor of Virginia began to hear rumors that the French were building forts along a route from the Great Lakes to the Ohio River system. That would tighten their hold on the Ohio Territory. The Virginia governor reported this to the English king, whose title was George III. The king ordered the governor to send an envoy into the Ohio Territory to warn the French off. If they refused to leave, the governor was to use force.

Who was he to send? Washington was young and inexperienced. And he was proud and hot-tempered. Through his life he always had to work hard to keep his temper under control. He also resented being disrespected. He once rode several hundred miles to protest another man being promoted over him in the military.

Washington was not the tactful sort of person usually named as an envoy. But he knew the wilderness and had shown that he could handle himself in rough country filled with Indians. So, he was sent, along with a small group to back him up.

Winter was coming. It would not be an easy trip. Once Washington reached the Ohio Territory, he went alone into the forest to find a good place for an English fort to be built. He picked a spot where two rivers joined to make the Ohio River. Later both the French and the British would build forts here. The British one was named Fort Pitt, after an English statesman, and eventually became Pittsburgh.

Washington then went on to meet with various French and Indian leaders, who lived in rough log forts and Indian villages. He told the French that King George wanted them to leave peaceably. As expected, the French refused. They intended to take over the territory themselves.

It was now December. Washington headed home. Eager to turn in his report, he hurried ahead with one of the party, a woodsman named Christopher Gist. They were joined by an Indian who offered to show them a shortcut. As they came into a glade in the forest the Indian suddenly dashed forward, swung around, and fired his musket at Washington. The bullet missed.

Washington and Gist charged at the Indian, tackled him, and flung him to the ground. Gist wanted to kill the Indian then and there, but Washington would not let him. It was typical of Washington: despite his many years as a soldier at war, Washington never liked killing. Later, as head of the American armies, he frequently had to punish spies and deserters. Sometimes he had them executed as an example to other soldiers; but in most cases he let them off.

The two travelers' troubles were not over. As they approached the last major river they had to cross, they expected to find it frozen over, so they could get to the other side. Instead, it was filled with chunks of ice. Washington and Gist built a raft and started across. Halfway over, Washington fell off into the freezing water.

He got back onto the raft, and eventually they reached a small island in the river. Incredibly, Washington slept that night, soaking wet, on the frozen ground. By morning the river had frozen over, and Washington and Gist made their way to safety.

The Virginia governor now had to make good on the British threat to drive the French out of the Ohio Territory. He put together a small force and asked Washington to command it. Washington rarely shrank from a challenge, but this time he knew he was far too inexperienced to command an attack force. He asked to be made second-in-command. The governor appointed another commander.

Meanwhile, the governor sent a workforce out to build a fort at the spot Washington had chosen. Then came news that the French had attacked the workers. The governor ordered Washington's troop to defend them. Unfortunately, the man who was supposed to command the group did not appear in time, and Washington was now in charge, whether he ought to have been or not.

Washington led a small force of 159 men into the wilderness. They soon met the work party heading back to Virginia. The workers told Washington that the French vastly outnumbered them and had told them to go home.

Now Washington discovered that there was a small French party in the woods nearby. His orders were clear enough: tell the French to leave, and only attack if they refused to. But Washington decided to do as the Indians did—mount a surprise attack.

An artist's version of Washington's small force attacking the French party, during which a diplomat was killed. The incident helped trigger the French and Indian War.

He did so. His troops killed ten of the French before they could surrender. It then turned out that the French party had been escorting a diplomat to Virginia with a message for the English governor. Unfortunately, the diplomat had been one of the men killed. This was indeed a serious matter: under rules of warfare then, diplomats and messengers were supposed to be allowed to proceed unharmed. Washington had made a serious mistake. But he was unfazed. He later said, "I heard the bullets whistle, and, believe me, there is something charming in the sound." Washington was now discovering that he liked to be in danger.

But the French were angry. They decided to teach the youthful commander a lesson. They dispatched a large force to deal with him. Learning that the French were coming, Washington built a wooden stockade in an open field for his defense, which he called Fort Necessity. Again Washington's rashness and inexperience showed. The stockade was too small to contain all his men, and there were high places around it from which the enemy could fire down into the fort from undercover.

This was exactly what the French and their Indian allies did. Instead of charging, they lay in the forested high ground and poured volley after volley into Fort Necessity. Washington's little army was cut to pieces. But Washington refused to give up. At nightfall he was still holding on, although it was clear that he could not last much longer.

Then the French offered to talk. Washington agreed to surrender, and the French quite graciously allowed him to take the remains of his little band home.

This small fight in the wilderness triggered by a headstrong young Virginian had important consequences in Europe. The British felt humiliated by the defeat. The French were violently angry about what they called the murder of their diplomat. The two countries were already hostile to each other, and Washington's rashness was tumbling them into war.

But to Virginians he was now a hero. He had won the battle against the French in which the diplomat had been killed and had held out for a day against a much stronger French force. He was becoming known as a brave and daring fighter.

The French now started to build a fort at the place Washington had picked earlier, where the two rivers met to form the Ohio. In response, the British sent Major General Edward Braddock with two regiments from England to take the French fort. Braddock had heard about the oversized, headstrong young Virginian and asked him to be his guide into the wilderness. Washington signed on as a civilian aide, not actually a member of the British army. He quickly warned Braddock that war in America was different from war in Europe. There, armies fought set battles in open areas, each army drawn up in precise formation. One army would charge down upon the other, firing as it came, and then, if not driven off, would fight hand-to-hand with bayonets.

In America the French had learned to fight Indian-style, taking enemies by surprise and fighting from behind trees and rocks.

Braddock had great faith in his men and in standard European tactics and he ignored the young man's advice. Instead he had his engineers cut a road through the forest, building bridges across streams and ravines. He advanced in military formation to within twelve miles of the French fort.

British general Braddock was used to fighting in the formal European way, with well-trained troops in disciplined ranks. Washington urged Braddock to fight as the Indians did, but Braddock would not. Here, a line of marching troops in brightly colored uniforms make easy targets.

Then the French and Indians struck, firing out of the forest. They slaughtered the unprotected British, who were brave but used to fighting in formation. The British tried to flee. Their officers attempted to organize them into the usual formations in the road they had been cutting. Washington urged Braddock to let him take some men into the woods and fight as the French were doing, but Braddock wouldn't let him. British officers, mounted on horses, made easy targets and were shot down. Braddock was seriously wounded. Washington had two horses shot from under him. His hat was shot off and his jacket was cut by bullets. But miraculously, he was not hurt.

When the Indians and French attacked from the cover of the woods, they easily picked off British officers on horseback, causing confusion in the ranks.

Soon Washington was the only one left capable of command, and he was really not in the army at all. He now led what remained of Braddock's force back along the road they had built, carrying the dying Braddock with them. In the end, Braddock ordered Washington to race back to Virginia to get help. Through the night, Washington rode, at times getting off his horse and crawling on hands and knees to find the way. The remains of the British force crept back into Virginia, carrying the body of General Braddock.

The battle had been a disaster for the British, but George Washington came out of it with a greater reputation than ever. He was seen as the hero who had urged Braddock to fight in the Indian way, and who had finally taken command and led the remaining troops to safety. And indeed it was a fair judgment. George Washington may have been rash, but nobody could question his courage nor his coolness under fire. The story of his role in the fight passed around the colonies. He was becoming a person known in America, and even a little in Europe. It was clear that not only did he like to be in danger, he liked to command. These were qualities that would have immense importance for the future of the United States.

Washington's role in Braddock's defeat made him a local hero in Virginia and to some extent elsewhere in America.

Chapter 3

A REBELLIOUS NATION PICKS A LEADER

THE ENGLISH AND THE FRENCH WERE now fully at war, not only in North America, but in Europe as well. This was what we call today the French and Indian War. The Indians generally sided with the French, with whom they had been trading for furs for some time. They also believed that the French would win. But neither side was able to strike a killing blow, and the war drifted on for several years.

This rough drawing, made not long after the battle, shows British troops scaling the cliff to reach the Plains of Abraham, where the critical fight for Quebec took place. The artist had obviously never visited the French capital. But such drawings were popular with the British, who were excited by their victory over the hated French.

Then a brilliant English statesman, William Pitt, took over in England. He sent a force to take the French capital of Quebec, which sat on a cliff high above the St. Lawrence River. British general James Wolfe brought his troops down the St. Lawrence and camped across the river from Quebec. For some weeks he attempted to find a way to get at the French in their cliff-top fortress. Then he noticed a tiny path going up the cliff just to the west of the town.

One night he slipped his men across the river in dead silence. They clambered silently up the cliff. In the morning the French found the British force in formation on the Plains of Abraham outside the city. There was a battle; the French were decisively beaten. In the peace treaty that ended the war the French agreed to turn Canada over to the English. Finally the Ohio Territory was cleared for American expansion. The effects on American history would be great.

Washington played no further role in the French and Indian War. For sixteen years, he would be a private gentleman tending to his estates. He married a widow, Martha Custis, who had a good deal of wealth from her first marriage. George was now able to live like the gentleman he aspired to be. He expanded his house, Mount Vernon, adding bedrooms and a ballroom. He bought more land to farm. He sent to England for the fashionable clothes, new furniture, and paintings, of the sort other Virginia gentleman had.

An artist's romantic idea of Washington's first meeting with his wife. In fact, marriages in those days were usually made for practical reasons. George and Martha had undoubtedly been social acquaintances before they decided to marry.

But proud as he was of his position, he was also a very smart businessman. He was out on his horse by sunrise seeing to things. He introduced new scientific methods of farming and improved his crops. He was also, as a Virginia gentleman, a member of the House of Burgesses, Virginia's legislature. Respected by everyone who knew him for his fairness and intelligence, he was always being asked to take on public jobs—vestryman of his church, justice in the local courts, officer in the militia.

Washington lived the life of a country squire. He was happy, always glad to welcome visitors—both he and his wife felt that life was dull unless they had people staying with them. But outside events would now shake that happiness.

Like many large Virginia estates, Mount Vernon was a small village, with its own blacksmith's shop, carpentry shop, slaves' quarters, and much else. The farmlands belonging to it ran for miles along the Potomac River.

The victory of the English over the French in the French and Indian War had important consequences. The French still had their foothold in New Orleans but were out of the Ohio Territory. The Spanish held the area around Florida, but were no immediate threat farther north. The Indians, without the support of their French allies, were becoming more cautious in attacking Americans on the frontier. Americans were coming to believe that they no longer needed the protection of the mighty British army and navy. Why, then, did Americans need to continue as servants to the British?

George Washington believed that in time the Americans would have to be free of the British control. However, he thought that was something for future generations to handle.

Other Americans did not want to wait. Particularly in Massachusetts, by the 1760s there was increasing talk of rebellion against England. The main problem was—as it so often is in politics—taxes. The British had run up large debts driving the French out of Canada. They were also maintaining outposts in the border lands to help control the Indians. Americans were getting many benefits from the British army; surely they ought to pay some of the costs.

That was reasonable enough. However, the British did not ask the Americans what they thought a fair share would be. They made the decisions in London and simply ordered Americans to cough up. Americans resented this. *No taxation without representation* became the cry: that is, Americans should not be taxed unless they had a voice in deciding how much they would pay.

It was a problem that reasonable men could have solved. And indeed there were in England many people sympathetic to the Americans, who could have worked out a compromise. But George III was a stubborn man who considered the colonists children who must obey him. Inevitably, he had for advisors people who believed the same.

George III, King of England

The Americans were not always reasonable either. There were of course many who did not want to break with England—perhaps a quarter of Americans wanted to remain loyal. But there were a good many Americans who saw the tax question as an excuse to rebel.

George Washington was not eager for a war that he assumed he would be drawn into. But he was also a man who did not shy from combat. And he was a man who liked to be in charge. In 1774 a call went out for representatives from all thirteen colonies to meet in Philadelphia to work out a plan of action against the British. Washington was chosen as one of the delegates from Virginia. Significantly, he wore his military uniform to the meeting. Was he trying to remind the other delegates that he had army experience? He never said.

We are now looking at a somewhat different George Washington from the headstrong young man who had welcomed battle at Fort Necessity. He was over forty, a married man with two step-children (he never had children of his own). He had held public office in Virginia. He had come to see that you could solve problems better if you did not simply follow your feelings but thought about the difficulty carefully. He also saw that it was important to know what others were thinking and feeling about the problem—not only to get their ideas, but to know what they were likely to do if this or that were done. He was now a good listener. Only when he had got all opinions and mulled them over in his mind for awhile would he come to a decision.

George Washington became internationally famous during the Revolutionary War. Many people asked to paint his portrait. He grumbled about the time the posing took, but was flattered enough to allow it.

This ability to put aside his first impulse and give himself time to consider a problem *rationally* proved to be one of George Washington's greatest strengths. He had learned self-control.

Thus, at the 1774 meeting, known as the First Continental Congress, Washington said little. Instead, he listened. For almost two months he met constantly with the delegates and other important people for tea, dinner, or supper, hearing what they had to say, and testing ideas. Because of his military feats twenty years earlier, he was well known to most of the delegates. They were glad to meet him, and most went away with a good impression of him.

By this time the British could see that the Americans were getting ready to rebel against them. They sent troops to Boston. And in April 1775 British soldiers marched out of Boston toward Concord, where the Americans had stored guns and ammunition. Massachusetts farmers were ready. At the little town of Lexington some shots were fired—by which side, nobody is sure.

Quickly the British drove off the Massachusetts men and marched on to Concord. They captured some of the guns and powder hidden there and turned to go back to Boston. Now the Americans began to pepper the British troops with gunfire from behind walls and barns and from inside houses. The British got back to Boston in much confusion. The American Revolution was on.

In May 1775 a second Continental Congress was held. It was clear to everybody that an American army had to be put together, and somebody named to command it. There was only one logical choice.

The first fighting in the Revolution took place when British troops met with American minutemen on the green in Lexington, Massachusetts, not far from Boston. Nobody is sure who fired the first "shot heard round the world." Once again, this artist's idea of the famous event is probably only roughly accurate.

Chapter 4

HARD LESSONS LEARNED

T HE HURDLES GEORGE WASHINGTON faced in building an army to fight the mighty British military machine were huge. The former colonies, now called states, were independent nations, with their own governments. They were joined by the Articles of Confederation, which established a national government in Philadelphia. But this government was exceedingly weak.

In the eighteenth century, modern musical instruments like trumpets with three valves and saxophones had not been developed. Armies marched mainly to drums, which could be heard for some distance, and shrill fifes, which also carried. The image of the fife and drummer has long been associated with the Revolution.

There was no president as we have today. Power lay with the Continental Congress, which, however, had no way to force the states to follow its orders.

Thus, the Congress would call upon the states to send Washington so many men, so much money, so many barrels of flour and gunpowder; the states would send what they pleased, or nothing at all.

The British had problems, too. For one, their supply base was England, three thousand miles away. Furthermore, a lot of English people did not like the war. For some it was a matter of principle: surely the Americans ought to have the same civil rights as Englishmen did. For others, who counted on American tobacco, cotton, timber, and furs for their businesses, the war was going to cost them money.

But George III was determined to bring the colonists back under his command. He sent a large force to America, which included mercenaries—rented troops, called Hessians, from the German principality of Hesse.

To a modern reader, used to war in which missiles can fly across continents in minutes, the Revolution appears to have been fought in slow motion. Washington took command in June 1775. He spent the next several months recruiting troops, training them, and gathering supplies. The British were also slow to get going; they did not like to fight in winter in any case. Not until the spring of 1776 was there any real action.

Washington took command of American troops after the Battle of Bunker Hill, when the British were still occupying Boston. By placing his cannon on high places around the city, he was able to force them out.

At first the British plan was to take the important port cities, choking off American business. Washington assumed that the British would strike New York. (New York City then occupied only the lower end of Manhattan. Much of the rest of present-day New York was farms and villages.) Washington set up his defenses in New York. Soon thereafter, on July 6, Washington received a copy of the Declaration of Independence, which gave the reasons why Americans ought to be free.

At almost the same moment the British fleet appeared in New York Harbor. The British had 30,000 trained and experienced soldiers against 23,000 mainly inexperienced and untrained Americans. Washington mounted a defense on Brooklyn Heights, across the East River from Manhattan. With a roar of gunfire the British attacked. The Americans panicked and fled. Washington was lucky to slip most of his men across the East river back to Manhattan under cover of darkness.

He now established a defensive line on a high point at the northern end of Manhattan. When the British landed lower down, Washington led some troops against them. Once again the Americans broke and ran at the sight of the bright red British uniforms. Washington rode among them shouting and striking at them with his whip, but the soldiers fled anyway.

The British soundly defeated the Americans in the Battle of Long Island. But Washington managed to save most of his troops by slipping them back across the East River into Manhattan at night, before the British knew what he was doing.

Soon Washington was alone on his horse facing the British army. Fifty British soldiers raced toward him. Washington faced them unmoved. Fortunately, some of his aides came running up and dragged him away. If they had not, this story would have ended right there, and so, probably, would have the American Revolution.

The British now took New York City without a struggle. They would hold it for the rest of the war. This accomplished, they turned northward to drive Washington's army away. However, this time the Americans, firing from behind trees and rocks, stood their ground; it was the British who fled. It had not been much of a battle, but at least the Americans had, for once, won.

But soon the Americans were driven off Manhattan Island. It was now plain that the British would attempt to capture Philadelphia, where the American government, such as it was, was located. The British general, William Howe, decided to build a string of forts through New Jersey. He believed this show of force would encourage New Jersey people to remain loyal to King George. With his base secured, he would then at his leisure cross the Delaware River and take Philadelphia.

But George Washington had by this time, in his deliberate manner, thought his way to his own long-range strategy. He saw clearly that the major problems were not military, but political. Many of the colonies were larger than whole European countries. They stretched for hundreds of miles along the Atlantic coast, much of the land forested and uncut by roads over which troops could march. The British might be able to take a town or city, even a whole small colony, but they could never hold all the colonies by force.

This well-known portrait shows Washington in his army uniform. He liked to dress in the finest of clothes when he could.

But that was true only if the bulk of Americans remained loyal to the patriot cause. If they began to lose heart, they would soon begin asking King George to forgive them, and it would all be over. The American leaders, like Washington, John Adams, Thomas Jefferson, and Benjamin Franklin, would be caught and hanged. Washington saw that he did not have to beat the British immediately. The main thing was not to be beaten himself; when he was losing, he would disappear to fight another day. Here again we see Washington's strength: in his heart he always wanted to fight, to attack; but his head told him to be cautious, and he would do what his mind, not his feelings, told him.

He continued to have trouble getting the men and material he needed from the government. In late 1776 he decided that an American victory would hearten people and encourage them to provide him with supplies. He would attack the British post at Trenton, New Jersey, just up the Delaware River from Philadelphia. It meant crossing the river in winter, always dangerous, but it was a risk he must take. He would attack on Christmas Day, when the Hessians, who were posted there, were likely to be sleeping.

On Christmas Eve the little army set out. A storm was blowing up and the temperature was dropping. The soldiers loaded themselves onto boats. The river was full of chunks of ice, which made poling the boats across difficult. The temperature continued to drop, and then a storm came on. A mixture of hail, snow, and freezing rain engulfed the men. Still, they struggled across. But progress was slow, and it was daylight before the American troops were over the river.

One of the most famous historical paintings in America shows Washington crossing the Delaware River to reach Trenton. It is not entirely accurate. For one thing, the boats were not rowed, but poled.

But the storm, however uncomfortable it made the men, covered the army's movements. The Hessians, snug and warm against the storm in Trenton, believed it was impossible for the enemy to move against them. When the Americans burst into Trenton firing, the Hessians were stunned. Their officers tried to organize them into their usual formations, but in the confusion and blinding snow it was impossible. The Hessians began to surrender. Soon it was over. Washington slipped his troops back across the Delaware, this time with nine hundred prisoners, some Hessian cannon, and wagons loaded with equipment.

A few days later Washington set his sights on the British garrison at Princeton, only a few miles north of Trenton. As he was marching his troops forward his advance guard bumped into two British regiments. The British quickly formed up in their usual fashion. Washington lined up his own men. Then he rode out in front of them, leading them toward the British. As they came within shooting distance, both sides fired. Incredibly, Washington was in between them, a large target on his horse. One of his aides in horror pulled his hat down over his eyes so as not to see his beloved commander killed. When he removed his hat Washington was still astride his horse, waving his troops on. This time it was the British who ran. Washington spurred his horse after them, and shortly Princeton was captured. Washington quickly took British supplies and prisoners and once again slipped away.

Chapter 5

THE WORLD TURNED UPSIDE DOWN

Georgeeorge Washington had been right: the victories at Trenton and Princeton gave the Americans a terrific boost in spirit. It now appeared that Americans could win, although nobody thought it would be easy. And Washington was certainly right in believing that the key to victory was to hold onto the support of Americans.

He ruled that citizens of New Jersey who had sworn allegiance to King George would be pardoned if they would now swear allegiance to the patriot cause. Many took advantage of Washington's offer.

Americans who sided with the British were called Tories. They were sometimes treated harshly by loyal Americans, as in this picture. But a great many Americans were Tories, and in general there was less hatred of them than might have been expected.

Those who refused were taken gently but firmly to the British lines, where most of them would spend the rest of the war.

Many loyal patriots were incensed that the Tories, as supporters of the king were called, had gone unpunished. Again Washington was right, for many Tories were grateful for Washington's leniency and no longer supported the British.

The victories at Trenton and Princeton were not huge, but they woke up Europeans and others to the fact that the rough American farmers might actually win. Most people everywhere lived under kings and dictators; the idea that a powerful ruler might be thrown off fascinated people, and eyes everywhere turned to the American Revolution.

One result was that a lot of European military officials crossed the Atlantic to see what was going on, and even to help. One of the best known of these was a Frenchman, the Marquis de Lafayette, a rich young man influential with French rulers. He and Washington quickly became great friends.

The Marquis de Lafayette was high in the French aristocracy. Charming and brave, he was a great favorite of Washington. In turn, Lafayette praised Washington to the French government, enouraging them to aid the Americans.

Another of these was a German with the imposing name of Friedrich Wilhelm Ludolf Gerhard Augustin Baron von Steuben. Von Steuben was an experienced drillmaster. Washington was wise enough to let von Steuben start training his troops in European tactics. Von Steuben soon learned that he could not handle the Americans as European troops were treated. The Europeans were trained to blindly obey orders. Von Steuben said that with the Americans you had to say, "This is the reason that you ought to do that," and then they'd do it.

The winter the American army spent at Valley Forge has always been remembered as a horrible time, with the soldiers going hungry and walking barefoot in the snow. At first it was, but bit by bit things improved, until conditions were not too bad.

The training soon made itself felt. In June 1778 Washington decided to attack a British army marching through an area near what was then called Monmouth Courthouse, in New Jersey. He sent one of his officers to the attack. The British fought back. The officer bungled the attack and soon the Americans were in retreat, with the British hotly pursuing them. When Washington got news of the disaster he spurred his horse forward. Lafayette later wrote, "General Washington seemed to arrest fortune with one glance . . . His presence stopped the retreat . . . His graceful bearing on horseback, his calm and deportment which still retained a trace of displeasure . . ." were enough to rally the troops. Lafayette added, "I thought then as now that I had never beheld so superb a man."

Rapidly Washington organized the troops. The British cavalry charged. The Americans held their fire until the cavalry was on them, and then broke the charge with a blast of gunfire. Next came the British infantry. The Americans held their ground, and then began to advance in proper military formation just as von Steuben had taught them. The British pulled back out of the fight.

We can see the importance of George Washington to the American Revolution. Where other commanders might have resented the foreigners coming to advise them, Washington put aside his natural pride and got what good he could from men like Lafayette and von Steuben.

Washington was not too proud to take advantage of help from experts. Von Steuben, shown here, was a great help in training American troops.

In turn, these people began reporting back to their friends in Europe that in George Washington the Americans had a great leader, a man who was wise and without fear. Support for the American cause grew.

This was particularly true of the French. They were always happy to see their rival, the English, suffer. It now seemed that the Americans could win, and the French decided to help. French troops and French ships began to trickle in. But despite everything, the war was far from won. The British took Philadelphia, and beat the Americans in a series of battles in the surrounding area. Then the British took the war into the South. Washington sent one of his best generals, Nathaniel Greene, into the South. Through Virginia and the Carolinas, Greene harassed the British force as best he could, but the British commander Lord Cornwallis was much too strong for Greene to drive away.

By 1781 Cornwallis was concentrating his forces in Virginia, where he had almost a free hand to do what he liked. He raided the Virginia legislature and captured some of its members. Virginia governor Thomas Jefferson fled into the mountains. He pleaded with Washington to come home and save his own state, but Washington knew that if he walked away from his army in the North the troops would quit the army and go home. As much as Washington loved the place where he had been born and had lived most of his life, he felt that his first duty was toward the new country he was helping to bring out of chaos.

Indeed, more and more the Continental Congress was treating Washington as if he were not merely commander of the American forces, but as if he were president. Again and again, Congress voted him powers to do this or that on his own best judgment.

In fact, to many it seemed as if the Revolution were not about America, but about Washington. The American representative in Paris announced that he had got a large sum of money for the American cause, which had been given because of "the exalted opinion" the French rulers had of Washington.

By 1781 the French had a large number of troops in America. It was time to take on Cornwallis. He was holed up on the York River in Yorktown, Virginia. The American and French troops began marching south from New York. At the same time a French fleet under Admiral de Grasse was sailing north from the West Indies to Chesapeake Bay. The idea was for the fleet to sail up the York River to Yorktown and bottle up the British troops there.

Washington had gone on ahead. When the French officers caught up with him, they saw an astonishing sight:

> *A tall officer in blue and buff regimentals was jumping up and down, waving in one hand a hat and in the other a white handkerchief. . . . The dancing figure seemed to be His Excellency, George Washington, but, of course, that was impossible. The Frenchmen knew that Washington was . . . of a natural coldness and of a serious and noble approach.*
> But it was Washington. He was shouting, "De Grasse, de Grasse," for he had learned that the French fleet was now in Chesapeake Bay. One of the French said later, "A child whose every wish had been gratified could not have been more happy."

The Americans and French now had Cornwallis out-numbered. The French fleet was in the river, preventing a British escape.

The French fleet held off the British ships sent to rescue Cornwallis's troops trapped in Yorktown, which led to the great American victory there.

The situation was much closer to what the British and the French were used to, with one army defending a fortified town, another attacking it from open ground. The attackers first bombarded the city, trying to destroy the fortifications and damage the troops inside. For two weeks the cannon pounded away, day by day destroying more and more of the fort.

Still Cornwallis hung on, hoping that the French fleet would be called away or that a British fleet would arrive to drive the French out. But they did not come.

Unable to get his troops out of Yorktown, Cornwallis knew he must surrender. Here, British troops march out to lay down their arms.

After two weeks the Americans stormed two British redoubts, or small fortifications, outside the town, which were quickly taken.

For another week the bombardment continued. Lord Cornwallis continued to cling to slim hopes. Finally he gave up. When the British marched out of Yorktown to lay down their arms, the American band played a song called "The World Turned Upside Down." Although nobody was sure of it just yet, the Americans, with the help of the French, had beaten the mightiest army in the world. And it is the belief of most historians that without the steady hand and sure judgment of George Washington as commander, it would not have happened.

Chapter 6

A NEW CONSTITUTION

T HE VICTORY AT YORKTOWN DID NOT quite end the American Revolution. The British still held New York City and had thousands of troops in North America, as well as a large fleet that might pounce at any time. But when news of Yorktown reached the British government, the king and his ministers despaired. English business-people in particular were tired of the vast amount of money going out and the interruption of trade

Although the British really stopped fighting after the surrender at Yorktown, peace negotiations dragged on. Not until November 1783 did Washington actually march his troops into New York City.

caused by the fighting. Public opinion was turning against the war. So the British government decided to give in, and negotiations for a peace treaty were begun in Paris.

The negotiations dragged on until 1783. In November of that year the British finally marched out of New York. George Washington could at last go home to his beloved, but badly neglected, Mount Vernon.

He was, however, leaving behind many problems. The Continental Congress had run up huge debts in fighting the Revolution. Not only did the new nation owe money to foreign lenders, but American soldiers, American farmers, American businesses had often gone unpaid for their services. How was this money to be raised?

For another matter, even though the British had signed a peace treaty, they were not living up to all the terms. Among other things, British soldiers were still in forts around the Great Lakes, at times encouraging the Indians to cause trouble. Besides the British, the Spanish in Florida were a threat. So, the new nation was facing not only the kinds of difficulties any nation faces, but all sorts of new ones that Americans had never had to deal with before. Unfortunately, the governmental system that had been hastily set up during the war was not up to the challenge. The basic problem was that it had no real power to do much of anything: the states wanted to keep power to themselves. They would not turn over to the national government the powers it needed to solve common problems. Many people continued to think of themselves as Rhode Islanders, Georgians, or New Yorkers, not as Americans.

Over the next few years it became clearer and clearer to thoughtful people that the national, or as we call it now, federal, government had to be strengthened or the union of states would fall apart. But could this be done?

Then, in 1786 an actual rebellion of farmers broke out in Massachusetts. These farmers were saddled with debt, often through no fault of their own. Courts were threatening to take their farms to pay off the debts. The farmers then began attacking the courts to prevent them from acting. The rebellion threatened to spread to other states where people had similar problems.

Shays' Rebellion, named after one of its leaders, was eventually put down by force, but it showed very clearly that the weak central government could not handle serious problems. Shays' Rebellion was a clear indication that something had to be done. Washington wrote a friend that change had to come "to avert the humiliating and contemptible figure we are about to make in the annals of mankind." James Madison wrote to James Monroe—both men would in time be president—"if the present paroxysm of our affairs be totally neglected, our case may become desperate."

But these more farsighted people knew that the majority of Americans were nervous about the idea of a strong central government. They had recently suffered much to rid themselves of an autocratic king; they did not want to put another harsh government over them. So Madison, Washington, and some others began quietly maneuvering to organize a convention of delegates from all thirteen states to create a new constitution. This would be the justly celebrated Constitutional Convention of 1787.

Washington did not really want to leave Mount Vernon; he had already spent too much time away from home. But from his wartime experience of dealing with a weak government, he knew better than anybody that improvement had to come. Furthermore, during eight years of war he had been the principal American leader. The country was his creation as much as it was anybody's, and he was determined to see it succeed. Finally, he knew that if he did not lend his prestige to the convention many others would stay away. When he arrived in Philadelphia, where the convention was to be held, he was automatically elected president of it.

This fanciful painting shows Washington making a speech at the Constitutional Convention. In fact, as president of the convention, he could not join the debates and spoke rarely. But his influence was felt behind the scenes.

The men at the Constitutional Convention had a great many difficult issues to settle. But two stand out. One was a conflict between the big states and the small ones. In the old Continental Congress each state had had one vote. The big states, like Virginia, Pennsylvania, and Massachusetts, felt this was unfair. Such states had many times the population of little states like Rhode Island and Delaware. They believed that surely the big states ought to have more votes than the little ones.

But the little states believed that if they allowed the big states to have more votes, the small states would be outvoted every time on matters important to them. Some of the big state delegates pointed out that the real conflict in America was not between the big and little states, but between the North and the South. But the little states would not give up. They said they would leave the convention if they didn't get their way.

As a big state man, Washington believed that the small states were wrong: a little state like Rhode Island shouldn't have an equal vote with a big one like Virginia. But to Washington, the most important thing was to get an agreement. It was part of his wisdom to understand that he couldn't always have things his way.

George Washington did not make many speeches at the Constitutional Convention. That was not his way. Instead he worked behind the scenes, meeting every day with other delegates to the convention at dinner, tea, or supper. He would listen carefully, and then present his ideas. In time a compromise was worked out. There would be a Senate, in which each state would

Chapter 7

THE FIRST PRESIDENT

GEORGE WASHINGTON WAS INDEED unanimously elected to be the first president under the new Constitution in 1789. He would not abuse his power, but he was determined to have a strong government. He took as his main ally his secretary of the treasury, the brilliant Alexander Hamilton, who also wanted a strong government. Hamilton worked out financial policies to encourage the development of manufacturing and a banking system that would

New York City was, for a brief period, the first capital of the new United States. Washington's arrival there to be sworn in as president was a great event, with cannons booming and ships swarming out to greet him.

help businesses to grow. Not everybody agreed with Hamilton's ideas. In particular, Thomas Jefferson, Washington's secretary of state, and James Madison both disliked cities and factories and wanted to keep America a rural nation devoted to farming. Nor did they want a very strong federal government, but hoped to see many decisions left to the states.

Thomas Jefferson was a friend and political ally of Washington, but opposed him on many points.

Like Jefferson, James Madison wanted a less powerful central government than Washington did. In the end, Washington's ideas won out.

But Washington took Hamilton's approach, and wherever possible tried to keep the federal government strong. For example, some people, particularly on the western frontier, objected to paying a tax on whiskey they made. They mobbed a few tax collectors. Washington tried to calm them by persuasion; but when that failed, he called out the militia and made a strong show of force. The rebellion melted away.

An even more important instance of Washington's wish for a strong presidency came in a conflict over a treaty with foreign powers negotiated by Washington's emissary, John Jay. The Jay Treaty was much disliked by many people. Congress wanted to overturn it, and demanded that Washington give it papers relating to the treaty. Washington refused to give Congress the papers, "because of the necessity of maintaining the boundaries fixed by the Constitution." The separation of powers, Washington believed, did not allow Congress to make this kind of claim on the president. When presidents today claim this principle, they call it "executive privilege."

Washington had one last thing to do for his country: retire. Many people wanted him to stay on as president for another term. At that time the Constitution allowed this. However, Washington knew he might die in office if he stayed too long. Then his vice president would take over.

If that happened, Washington thought, other presidents might decide that they, too, ought to stay in office until they died. Presidents would become like kings, passing their office along to their handpicked vice presidents.

Washington wanted to show that in the United States there could be a peaceful change of leaders, with the old president giving way to the new one after an election. So, after eight years he retired. In 1797 a new election was held. John Adams was elected president after a bitter fight. But he took over without any objections. Once again, Washington had done the right thing. Ever since, our newly elected presidents have taken over peacefully.

This portrait of Washington, done as his presidency was ending, shows him weary from so many years of responsibility, but nonetheless determined to do what was best for the nation.

What, finally, can we say about George Washington? The first thing is that he was no man of marble. He sometimes lost his temper, he was quick to jump into battle, he liked nothing better than a day spent on horseback followed by a jolly dinner with friends and family.

But George Washington had a passion for what was in those days called *fame*. Today people become famous for being good athletes, well-known musicians, popular actors. In Washington's time, fame meant something like *lasting honor.* A person could not become famous simply because he could hit a baseball far or sing in a popular style. He or she had to do something that was really important to a nation or the world.

Washington had no children of his own, but was devoted to the children of his wife, Martha, from her first marriage. He enjoyed his home life very much.

Washington believed that if he helped to found a great nation he would earn undying fame. To do so he knew he had to be wise. He had to think things through, rather than follow his first impulses.

Even though he was always eager to attack, during the Revolution he again and again held back until he had a good chance to win. At the Constitutional Convention he wanted a strong government, but he also knew that he would have to compromise to get the Constitution accepted. As president he frequently bided his time, refusing to cross bridges he had not yet come to, until he saw a way to resolve the problem.

This then is the reason why George Washington seems so much like a statue of cold marble: it was not that he lacked feelings, but that he had learned not to act on them until he was sure he was doing the right thing. Always he would listen to all sides of every question, consider what everybody said very carefully, and then make his decision. Historians today are astonished by how often he was right. George Washington was a great man because he *willed* himself to be one. He was not born to greatness; he made his way there step by step.

This famous sculpture of Washington was made at Mount Vernon not long after the end of the Revolution. His family thought it the most accurate depiction of him. The sculptor based it on a mask he applied to Washington's face.

This map shows some of the places important in Washington's life and to the fighting in the American Revolution. The insert shows detail of New York City, where Washington's army fought the British.

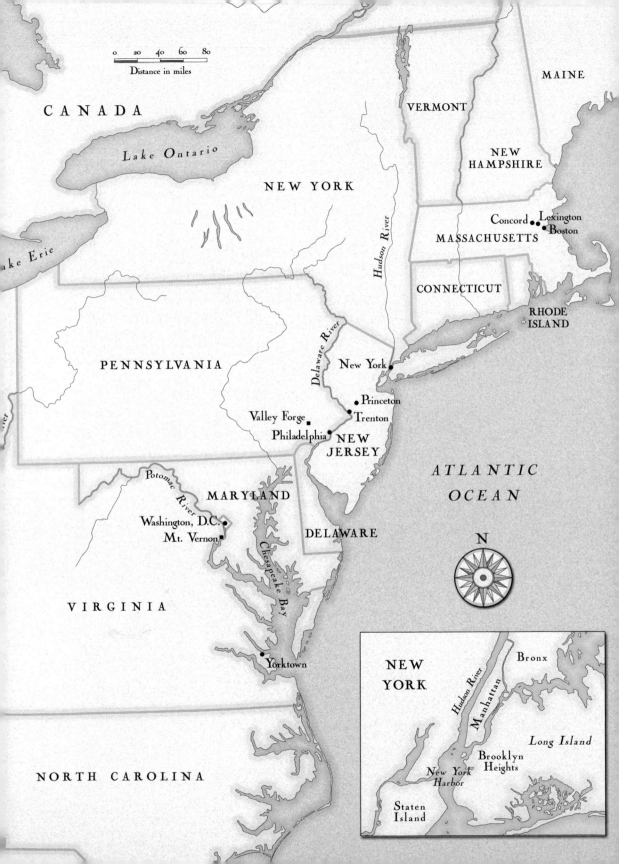

AUTHOR'S NOTES ON SOURCES

The amount of material currently available on George Washington is staggering. Perhaps the most valuable one volume study is *George Washington: The Indispensable Man*, by James Thomas Flexner. Material for younger students is less abundant. A useful volume is *George Washington and the Founding of a Nation*, by Albert Marrin. There is also *George Washington and the Birth of Our Nation*, by Milton Meltzer.

Flexner, James Thomas. Washington: *The Indispensable Man*. Boston, Little Brown, 1969.

Marrin, Albert. *George Washington and the Founding of a Nation*. New York, Dutton, 1997.

Index

ABOUT THE AUTHOR

James Lincoln Collier has written many books, both fiction and nonfiction, for children and adults. His interests span history, biography, and historical fiction. He is an authority on the history of jazz and performs weekly on the trombone in New York City.

My Brother Sam Is Dead was named a Newbery Honor Book and a Jane Addams Honor Book and was a finalist for a National Book Award. *Jump Ship to Freedom* and *War Comes to Willy Freemen* were each named a notable Children's Trade Book in the Field of Social Studies by the National Council for Social Studies and the Children's Book Council. Collier received the Christopher Award for *Decision in Philadelphia: The Constitutional Convention of 1787*. He lives in Pawling, New York.